NEW EDITION
Wide Range Readers
GREEN BOOK 2

Fred J. Schonell
Phyllis Flowerdew

Oliver & Boyd

Illustrated by Moira Chesmur, Pamela Goodchild, Hilary McElderry, Carol Holmes, Harry Horse, Peter Joyce, Maggie Ling, and Sheila Smith.

Oliver & Boyd
Longman House
Burnt Mill
Harlow
Essex CM20 2JE

An Imprint of Longman Group UK Ltd

First published 1950
Second edition 1965
Third edition 1976
Fourth edition 1985
Fifth impression 1990

© Phyllis Flowerdew and the Executors of the late Sir Fred J. Schonell 1965, 1985.
(Except 'The Very Funny House' © Elizabeth Casciani 1985; 'Choosy Susie and the New Shoes' and 'The Rainbow Scarf' © Daphne Lister 1985; 'Silas the Snake Does a Good Turn' © Anne Leask 1985; and 'Class 4's Summer Outing' © Moira Miller 1985.)

All rights reserved; no part of this publication may be reproduced, stored in a retrieval system or transmitted in any form or by any means, electronic, mechanical, photocopying, recording, or otherwise without either the prior written permission of the Publishers or a licence permitting restricted copying in the United Kingdom issued by the Copyright Licensing Agency Ltd, 33-34 Alfred Place, London, WC1E 7DP.

ISBN 0 05 003750 1

Set in 14/20pt Monophoto Plantin
Produced by Longman Group (FE) Ltd
Printed in Hong Kong

Preface

The Wide Range Readers are planned to provide graded reading practice for junior school children. Because children of 7–11 have a wide range of reading needs and attainments, there are three parallel series—Blue, Green and Red books—to provide plenty of material to suit the interests and reading ages of every child.

Books 1–4 are graded by half yearly reading ages, for use by appropriate groups within a class. Book 1 should provide an easy read for children with a reading age of about 7–7½. Children with reading ages below 7 are recommended to use the Wide Range Starters.

The controlled vocabulary of the series makes the books suitable for the following reading ages:

6½–7	**Starter Books**—Blue, Green and Red
7–7½	**Book 1**—Blue, Green and Red
7½–8	**Book 2**—Blue, Green and Red
8–8½	**Book 3**—Blue, Green and Red
8½–9	**Book 4**—Blue, Green and Red
9+	**Book 5**—Blue, Green and Red
10+	**Book 6**—Blue, Green and Red
11+	**Book 7**—Red only
12+	**Book 8**—Red only

Acknowledgments

We are grateful to the following for supplying photographs and giving permission for their use: Douglas Corrance, cover; Mary Evans Picture Library, p. 37; Scala, p. 5.

Where to Find the Stories

page

5	Saint Francis and the Wolf
14	The Very Funny House
24	Choosy Susie and the New Shoes
29	Silas the Snake does a Good Turn
37	The Girl who Sang
49	Shining Moon and his Toy Canoe
66	The Lazy Donkey
70	The Jigsaw Puzzle
83	The Rainbow Scarf
89	Blackie
104	Hot Supper
116	Class 4's Summer Outing

Saint Francis and the Wolf

Long ago in Italy
there lived a man named Francis.
He was so kind and gentle that
everyone loved him, and he
later became known as Saint Francis.
Even the birds and animals knew
he was their friend.   Birds would fly
down to him from the sky,
and fishes would come to the top
of the water, to listen to his words.

Now Saint Francis once went to stay
in a city where there was a fierce wolf.
The wolf stole sheep and lambs for food.
It was so fierce that it sprang
upon people in the street.
Mothers wouldn't let their children
go out to play. Men carried sticks
and swords when they went to their work.
No one dared to walk
on the hillside outside the city.
Everyone hated the cruel wolf,
and everyone was afraid of it.

Saint Francis was sorry
to find the people unhappy and afraid.
So he said,

"I'll go out and see this wolf."

"No, no. It will kill you,"
said his friends. They tried to stop
him from going, but Saint Francis said,

"Let me go. I'm not afraid."

The people went a little way
along the street with him.

Then they waited, and watched him
go on alone up the green hillside.

Almost at once the wolf came running
to Saint Francis. Its mouth was open,
and its white teeth looked sharp
and cruel. Just as it was about
to spring upon him, Saint Francis
stretched out his hand, and said softly,

"Come here, Brother Wolf.
Don't hurt me."

The fierce wolf closed its mouth,
and sat down at his feet,
as a friendly dog might have done.

"Brother Wolf," said Saint Francis,
"you've been very bad.
You've killed animals and men.
You've made everyone hate you.
You've been cruel and wicked."

The wolf pricked up his ears as if
he were listening. Then he hung
his head as if he were ashamed.
Then Saint Francis said,

"Brother Wolf, I want to make peace
with you. I know that you were cruel
because you were hungry.
If I see that the people of this town
give you food every day,
will you promise me that you'll
never hurt a man or an animal again?"
The wolf nodded his head.

"Will you promise me this,
Brother Wolf?" said Saint Francis again.

The wolf nodded his head.
Then he lifted up his paw, and put it
into the hand of Saint Francis.
This was his promise.

"Come then, Brother Wolf,"
said Saint Francis. "Let's go
into the city and tell the people."

So Saint Francis walked back
into the city, and the wolf trotted
beside him like a dog.

How surprised the people were to see
the fierce wolf walking so tamely
beside Saint Francis.

In a little while everyone
had heard the news.   Crowds
of people went to the market-place
to see the strange sight.

Saint Francis put his hand
on the wolf's head,
and spoke to the people.

"Listen," he said.

"Brother Wolf has made a promise to me.
If you will give him food every day,
he'll not hurt you or your children
or your animals. Will you promise
to feed him every day?"

"Yes," shouted the people.

"Brother Wolf," went on Saint Francis,
"will you make your promise
before all these people?"

Again the wolf nodded his head,
and put his paw
in the hand of Saint Francis.

So the wolf lived in the city,
and the people fed him. He kept
his promise, and they kept theirs.

The wolf went from door to door,
walking in and out of the houses
as he wished. The people patted him
and talked to him, and the children
played with him in the sunshine.
So the wolf became friendly and gentle,
and everyone loved him.

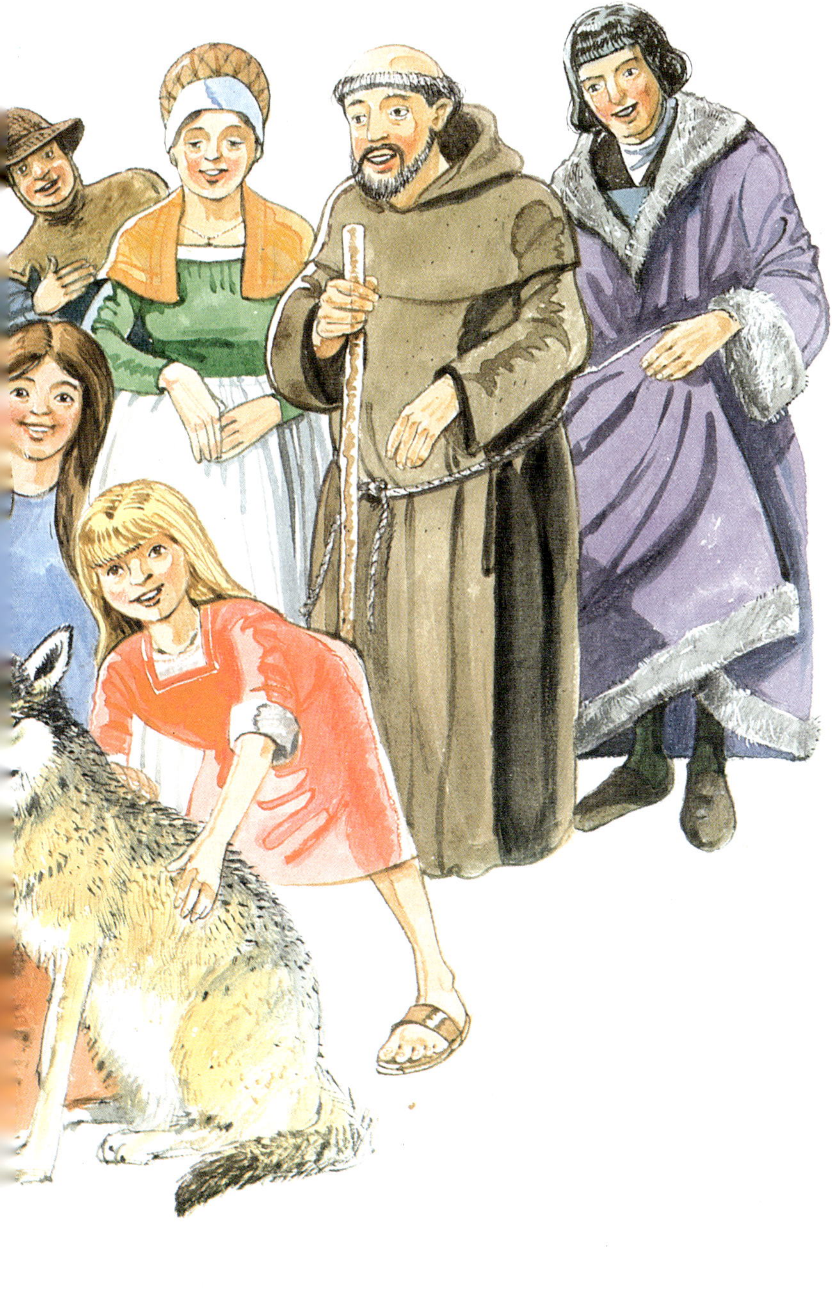

The Very Funny House

One morning a new girl
came to Jenny's school.
Jenny was painting a picture
when her teacher said,
 "Jenny, this is Muneera. She hasn't
been to this school before.
Would you like to take care of her?"
Jenny smiled. So did Muneera.
 "Hello," Muneera said.
"What are you doing?"

"I'm painting a picture of
my house," said Jenny.   "This is
the door.   That's the window downstairs.
That's my bedroom window on top."

"I'd like to do that too," Muneera said.

Jenny gave her new friend
a big piece of paper and a brush.
Muneera picked up a pot
of purple paint.   Jenny looked puzzled.

"Houses aren't purple," she said.

"Mine is," Muneera told her.
"And it's got a big yellow stripe
round the middle."   She took a pot of
yellow paint and Jenny laughed.
Muneera was a funny girl.

"I need black for the wheels,"
Muneera said.   "Can I use that black?"
Jenny gave her the black paint and
laughed again.

"Houses don't have wheels."

"Mine does," said Muneera and they both
laughed and laughed.

When she had finished, Jenny said,
"I'm going to do another painting.
I'm going to paint my bedroom."

Muneera watched as she painted
a pink carpet and a brown bed.
At the top of the paper
Jenny put a big pink splodge
for the lamp shade.

"It's new," she told Muneera,
"with flowers on it."

"Now I'll do my bedroom," said Muneera.
"There's the bed and there's the window."

Jenny looked puzzled.

"That's upside down. Beds don't go on the ceiling."

"Mine does," Muneera said and Jenny could hardly stop laughing.

They painted together all morning. Soon they were very good friends. Every day they did their work together. When it was time for milk they sat together. They looked at books in the book corner together.

Best of all, Jenny liked to paint pictures with Muneera because Muneera's pictures were so funny.

One day Muneera said,
"Would you like to come to my house for my birthday tea party?"

"Oh yes, please," Jenny smiled. "But I don't know which street you live in."

"I don't live in a street," Muneera laughed. "I live in a car park." Jenny began to giggle. Muneera was a very funny friend.

"I'll get my mum to tell your mum where we live so that you can come," Muneera promised.

Jenny was delighted. That very day their two mums talked together. Jenny's mum said they would be at Muneera's house at three o'clock on Saturday.

On Saturday afternoon Jenny and her mum set off for Muneera's house. Mum said it was a long way,

so they took the bus.
Jenny could hardly wait as the
bus drove through the town.
At last Mum said it was time to
get off. Jenny was surprised.
There were no houses in this part
of the town, but across the road
there was a large garage
and a car park.

"Here we are, Jenny," said Mum.

They crossed the road and walked round
to the back of the garage.

There in front of them was
a large, purple caravan. It had a
yellow stripe round the middle and
standing at the door was Muneera.

"Hello, Jenny," she called. "Come in."

Jenny was so surprised she
almost forgot to say "Happy Birthday"

until her mum pointed to the
parcel she was carrying and said,
 "Give Muneera her present, Jenny."
 "Happy Birthday, Muneera," Jenny said.
"You *do* have a purple house with
a yellow stripe round the middle."
 "And black wheels," Muneera laughed.
"This is my dad's new garage.

We're staying here in the caravan
till Dad finds us a house.
I hope we come to live near you."

"So do I," Jenny said.

Inside the caravan Muneera's mum
had put a beautiful birthday cake
on the table. It had seven pink
candles on it. They had a lovely tea.

When they had finished, Jenny helped to
clear all the dishes into the
tiny caravan kitchen and watched
Muneera's mum fold the table and
put it in a cupboard
to make space for them to play.

"May I show Jenny my bed?"
Muneera asked.

"All right," her mum said.
She put her hand up to the
ceiling and pulled a leather strap.
In a minute a beautiful bunk bed
unfolded and Muneera showed Jenny
how to climb up a wooden ladder.

"Your bed *is* on the ceiling," Jenny said in amazement.

Later, when it was time to go home, Jenny looked round the cosy caravan.

"I don't think you need a new house, Muneera," she whispered. "I think your purple caravan with the yellow stripe and black wheels is lovely."

And they both laughed and laughed.

Elizabeth Casciani

Choosy Susie and the New Shoes

Susie needed some new shoes.
Her old ones nipped her toes
and they had a big hole in
them too.

"We'll go and buy a new pair
this afternoon," said her mother.

"I don't want black and I don't want buttons and I would like some that make a nice sound when I walk," said Susie.

"Choosy Susie," her brother teased.

When they got to the shop there were so many pairs of shoes to choose from! Susie found it very hard to make up her mind.

There were brown shoes that made her think of the shiny chestnuts

that she and her brother had collected
in the park in autumn.

There were white shoes—as white
as the snow that had fallen in
winter-time.

There were blue shoes almost exactly
the same colour as her dad's car.

There were red shoes like
the pillar box outside Susie's house
where she sometimes posted letters for
her mum and dad.

Some shoes had buttons, some
had laces, some had buckles
and some had bows.

Susie liked them all. She didn't know
which pair to have.

Then she saw a pair of
shiny black shoes, just like the blackbird
who came to sing outside their
kitchen window every day. They had
shiny black buttons, just like the
blackbird's bright, beady eyes.

"That's the pair I like best,"
said Susie.

"But you said you didn't want black,"
her mother reminded her. "And you said
you didn't want buttons."

"I've changed my mind," said Susie.

"Choosy Susie," her brother teased again.

Susie tried on the black shoes.
They were just the right size.
She walked up and down in front
of the mirror in the shop.
Yes, *they* were the shoes she wanted.

"Please may I keep them on
to go home?"

"All right," said her mother.

Mother paid for the shoes and
got the change. Then they left
the shop. When Susie walked outside in
the street the shoes said, "Tap, tap, tap,"
very softly.

"They make a nice sound," said Susie,
smiling. "I like these shoes best of all."

"Choosy Susie," her brother said.

Daphne Lister

Silas the Snake does a Good Turn

Silas was a slippery, slithery brown snake.
He lived in the jungle, in a
banana tree with big, feathery leaves.
He would coil himself round the tree
till he looked just like a
twisted brown branch.   Then he would
unwind his coils, and hang down,
like a long, brown rope, to watch
the monkey children playing football
with a round, hairy coconut.

His bright, beady eyes glittered with
excitement. His forked tongue flicked in and
out of his mouth. He longed to
join in their games, but whenever
he came too near, Mother Monkey said
to her children,

"Run along now, no more football!
Silas is here—and snakes can bite,
you know!"

It was the same when he slithered
through the tall bamboo canes,
where the tiger cubs played hide-and-seek.
When their mother saw Silas, she growled,

"Look out! Here comes Silas!"
Then they all scampered away.

Even when Silas slid up the
trunk of a tree, the parrots scolded,
chattering a warning to each other,
and flew off to another tree.

Poor Silas just couldn't understand it
at all. He *certainly* didn't want to
bite anyone! All *he* wanted was someone
to play with, for he often
felt very lonely.

One hot day, all the animals
in the jungle were having an
afternoon nap. The monkeys were
sound asleep under a coconut palm.
Silas was curled up in a fork
of the banana tree, dozing peacefully,
and there wasn't a sound to be heard.

Suddenly, Silas was awakened by a soft,
whimpering noise near by. Had he been
dreaming? No, there it was again,
high up in the banana tree.

He lifted his smooth, flat head and
stared with his glittering, beady eyes.

There, at the top of the tree
was Matilda, the youngest of
Mother Monkey's children.
She was clinging to a very thin
branch, which *had* been laden
with bananas, and looked as if it were
going to break any moment.
She was all alone, shivering with
fright as she looked down at the ground.

It seemed to be an awfully long way down.

"What *are* you doing up there, Matilda?" asked Silas curiously. "You're *much* too small to be at the top of a big tree all by yourself!"

Matilda looked ashamed.

"Well, you see," she explained, "I felt hungry, and the bananas on this tree are so delicious I thought I would have a little snack while everybody else was asleep." She rubbed her tummy. "Oh, dear, I *wish* I hadn't eaten so many bananas! I really don't feel very well. And I don't know *how* I'm going to get down from this branch!"

"Don't worry, Matilda," said Silas soothingly. "We'll think of something."

He scratched his head with the tip of his tail, and thought hard for a minute or two. Then he had an idea.

"I'll twist my tail round the branch where you're sitting," he said, "and hang down as far as I can stretch, like a long rope.

Then you can slide down right to the ground."

Matilda cheered up. That sounded great fun! She watched eagerly while Silas flicked his tail beside her, knotting it tightly round the branch. Then the rest

of him slid down the tree, till
his head was almost on the ground.

"Now then," he told her,
"ready, steady, go!" Matilda gripped his
slippery, scaly body tightly with her
little pink hands. "Oh, what good
fun this is!" she cried.
And with a whoosh she was at
the bottom of the tree,
just as her mother was waking up
from her nap.

"Where *have* you been, Matilda?" asked
her mother crossly. "How often have I
told you never to go away
by yourself? Silas might find you!"

"But, Mother," said Matilda, "that's
exactly what happened. Silas *did* find me,
and brought me safely back!"

Silas was busy untying the knot
in his tail when Mother Monkey came to
thank him for helping Matilda.

"I'm sorry we've been so unkind
to you, Silas," she said,
"but please come and drink some
coconut milk with us, and we'll
be friends."

After that, Silas often gave swings
to the monkey children, and tied knots
in his tail to amuse them.
And he was never lonely again.

Anne Leask

The Girl who Sang

Many years ago in Sweden,
there was a little girl who sang.
She sang with the birds as they chirped
in the hedges.   She sang with the wind
as it sighed in the trees.   She sang
in time to her own footsteps
as she skipped along the country lanes.

In 1828, when she was nearly
eight years old, she moved to a house
in the town. The house stood in
a busy street where many people passed.
They hurried to and fro
on their way to the shops,
or the theatre, or their work.
The little girl wanted to sing
but here in the busy town there were
no birds chirping, and no trees near by.
So the little girl sang to her cat.
She sat him in the window,
and tied a pink bow round his neck,
and then she sang to him.

A man passing by on his way to work
heard the sound of singing. He looked up
and saw a little girl with fair, reddish hair,
a snub nose and grey eyes
—and he saw her cat.
He smiled and said to himself,

"I've never heard anyone sing so beautifully
as that little girl sings to her cat."

Next came a woman
with a shopping basket. She heard
the sound of singing. She looked up
and saw the little girl and her cat.
She too smiled and said to herself,

"I've never heard anyone sing
so beautifully as that little girl
sings to her cat."

Then came a lady who was a maid
to one of the dancers in the theatre.

She heard the sound of singing.
She looked up and saw the little girl
and her cat.
She smiled and said to herself,
   "I've never heard anyone sing
so beautifully as that little girl
sings to her cat."

Soon all the people who passed along
that street day after day began to know
that house.   They would walk more slowly
when they came to it.   They would look
up and smile at the cat
with the pink ribbon round his neck,
and at the little girl who sang to him.

They would listen with delight to her songs.
They would listen in wonder
to the music of her voice.

Now one day, (for this is a true story)
the lady who was a maid to a dancer
at the theatre said to the dancer,

"Every day in a house that I pass,
there's a little girl
sitting in the window with a cat.
The cat wears a pink ribbon round his neck,
and the little girl sings to him.
She has a wonderful voice.
I've never heard anyone sing
so beautifully as that little girl
sings to her cat."

"Find out who she is," said the dancer.
"Ask her mother to bring her to me,
so that I may hear her sing."

So the dancer's maid found out the name
of the little girl.

It was Jenny Lind.

Then Jenny Lind went with her mother

to sing at the dancer's house.
Jenny's hair was brushed and shining,
and her grey eyes were big
with excitement. She felt very shy
and a little frightened at first
but the dancer talked to her kindly
for a while. Then she said,
 "Will you sing to me now,
just as you sing to your cat?"
 So Jenny Lind stood
in the middle of the room, and sang,
just as she sang to her cat.
All the room was filled
with the music of her voice.
 "She's wonderful!" said the dancer
to Jenny's mother. "She's wonderful.
You must have her trained
to go on the stage."
 "No," said Jenny's mother.
"I don't want her to go on the stage."
 "But at least you must let her
have singing lessons," said the dancer.

"I'm glad that she sings so well,"
replied Jenny's mother,
"but I'm poor, and I've no money
to pay for singing lessons."

"Listen," said the dancer.
"Take Jenny to the singing master
at the Royal Theatre, and let her sing
to him. I'll give you a letter
for him. He may be able to help you."

How excited Jenny was now!
She and her mother walked through
the town to the Royal Theatre.
Mother held the letter tightly,
and Jenny hummed to herself
as she skipped along the street.

Soon they came to the Royal Theatre.
It was very large and very grand.
Once more Jenny felt shy and
a little frightened. Up the wide
steps they went, up and up.
Then Mother stopped halfway.
"I don't think we'll go," she said.

"Oh, yes, yes," begged Jenny,
tugging at her hand. So they
came in a few moments to the room
where the singing master sat.
He was a big man with black, curly hair.
He read the letter Jenny's mother
gave him. Then he said to Jenny,

"I should like to hear you sing."

So Jenny Lind stood
in the middle of the room and sang,
just as she sang to her cat.

The whole room was filled
with the music of her voice.
"She's wonderful!"
said the singing master
to Jenny's mother.
"I'll take her at once
to the head of the theatre,
and let her sing to him."

The singing master took Jenny
to another room, where
the head of the theatre sat.

"I've brought a little girl to sing
to you," said the singing master.
The head of the theatre glanced down
at Jenny, and she looked so small
that he was quite cross.

"This is no place for babies!" he said.
"This is the Royal Theatre—
the King's theatre."

Jenny was so shy that she tried
to hide herself
behind the kind singing master.

The singing master was angry
because the head of the theatre
wouldn't hear her sing.

"If you won't listen to her,"
he cried, "I'll teach her myself,
and she'll not pay me a penny
for her singing lessons.
Then one day she'll amaze you!"

"All right," said the head
of the theatre more kindly.
"I'll hear her."

So Jenny Lind stood
in the middle of the room and sang,
just as she sang to her cat.
All the room was filled
with the music of her voice.

"She's wonderful,"
said the head of the theatre
to the singing master. "I've heard
hundreds of people sing, but I've
never heard anyone sing so beautifully
as this little girl. You've surely
found a treasure!"

From that day Jenny Lind
was given singing lessons
at the Royal Theatre in Sweden,
and when she grew up she became
one of the most famous singers
in the world—all because,
when she was a little girl,
someone saw her sitting in the window
singing to her cat.

Shining Moon and his Toy Canoe

Once upon a time in North America
there was a little Indian boy
whose name was Shining Moon.
His wigwam stood in the forest
where the Splashing River flowed.
He lived in the wigwam
with his mother and father
and baby sister.

His father went out hunting.
His mother stayed at home
and cooked and sewed.
His baby sister swung in her cradle
from the branch of a tree.
But Shining Moon played outside
the wigwam, or down on the banks
of the Splashing River.
He was as happy as the squirrels
climbing in the trees.
He was as happy as the fish swimming
in the deep, grey water.
He was as happy as the birds flying
in the wide, blue sky.

Shining Moon had many toys
which his father had made for him.
He had a ball made of fur
and little animals made out of wood.
But better than these he liked his
toy canoe and his little bow and arrow.
The canoe was made of tree bark,
with a long string tied to one end.

Shining Moon always held tightly
to the string when he floated the canoe.
He didn't want the Splashing River
to carry it away.

His bow and arrows were made
of birch twigs, and he liked to try
shooting at trees with them.
When he grew older, he would
be able to go hunting with his father.

One day Shining Moon went to the edge
of the Splashing River to play
with his canoe. Gently he set it down
on the water, and ran along the bank
beside it, holding the string.
The river was calm near the edge.
There were many tree roots
reaching out and catching the weeds
that came by.

"I think," said Shining Moon to himself,
"that I'll let my canoe sail down alone,
just once. The tree roots will stop it
from going too far."

So he untied the string and let
the little boat sail all alone.
Down along the edge of the river it went
—bobbing up and down.
Shining Moon ran along beside it
until a tree root stopped it.
Then Shining Moon
took the boat out of the water
and walked back
to where he had started.

"It goes much better by itself,"
he thought. "I'll let it go
once more." So he went on playing
with his toy canoe, letting it sail
by itself again and again.

But soon a little wave
caught it and carried it away
from the edge. Before Shining Moon
could get it, it was out of reach.
It floated swiftly away
down the middle of the Splashing River.

"Oh!" cried Shining Moon. There was
nothing he could do to save it,
for the river was deep,
and he couldn't swim. He just watched
the little canoe floating bravely
down the river—away and away
and out of sight!
He ran beside the river
for a few minutes, but he knew
it was no use,
and he turned slowly back again.

He had lost his little canoe
made of tree bark.
He would never, never see it again!

He was very sad.
He was as sad as the wind that cried
round the wigwam in the cold winter.
He was as sad as the birds when they
could find nothing to eat in the snow.
His little canoe had gone.

For a long time he stared
at the Splashing River.   Then he said,

"I still have my bow and arrows.
I'll play with those."

First he tried shooting at the trunk
of a tree.   Then he thought of a new game.

"I'll shoot one arrow," he said.
"Then I'll run to it, and shoot again
from the place where it lands.
I'll follow the arrow and see where it
takes me."

So he turned his back to the river,
and stood with his feet apart.

He fitted an arrow to the bow,
and let it fly.
Whizz! It shot through the air,
and landed a good way ahead,
among the trees.
Shining Moon ran to pick it up.
Then he stood
facing the way the arrow pointed,
and he let it fly again.
"This is a good game," he said.
"I'll call it the Arrow Hunt."

So he played in the morning sunshine.
He shot an arrow and ran to pick it up.
Then he shot it again and ran after it.
He was so pleased with the new game
that he didn't see that he was
going further and further away
from his wigwam and the Splashing River.
He didn't see that he was going
deeper and deeper into the forest.

Sunbeams and shadows danced
among the trees.
Again and again flew the arrow,
silver in the sunlight.
On and on ran Shining Moon,
further and further away from the wigwam
and the Splashing River
—deeper and deeper into the forest.

Suddenly Shining Moon felt hungry.
He picked up the arrow and turned
to go home.   But the forest trees
were not the forest trees he knew.
He didn't know which way to go.

He was lost. He stood still and stared
at a squirrel that moved the leaves
above his head.
Shining Moon was sad.
He was as sad as the wind that cried
round the wigwam in the cold winter.
He was as sad as the birds when they
could find nothing to eat in the snow.
Shining Moon was lost.

"This is an unlucky day," he thought.
"I've lost my little canoe
in the Splashing River,
and I've lost myself in the deep
green forest."

He wanted to cry, but he knew
that Indian boys should never cry,
so he thought hard instead.

"I don't know which way to go,"
he said, "so I'll look for the sun."
Shining Moon looked through the trees.

"Ah, there it is," said Shining Moon.
"In the morning I see the sun
over there from my wigwam.
I'll walk back this way."
He walked in and out between the trees.
He walked through the sunbeams
and the shadows.
He walked and walked and walked.

The sun rose high in the sky,
till it was right overhead.

"It's midday," said Shining Moon.

The sun went down a little
towards the West.

"It's afternoon," said Shining Moon.

The sun went down a little more
and the shadows of the trees
grew long and thin.

"It's evening," said Shining Moon.
He wondered if he would
ever find his way home.

Then he heard a noise.
He stood still and listened.
It was a splashing, splashing sound.
It must be the Splashing River.

"Oh!" cried Shining Moon.
"If I can get to the river,
then I'll know my way home."

He ran through the forest,
in and out among the trees,
on and on over the long shadows
and the last sunbeams.
He came out
beside the Splashing River.

"Oh!" cried Shining Moon with joy.
"Now I'll be all right.   Our wigwam
is beside the Splashing River.
If I follow the Splashing River,
then I'll find my way home."

But then he thought of something else,
something that made him sad again.
Here was the Splashing River
with tree roots reaching out
to catch the weeds that came by.

But this wasn't the part
of the Splashing River that he knew.
Which *way* was his wigwam?
Should he go to the right,
or should he go to the left?
He didn't know.
He was still lost after all.

   He stood on the bank and stared
at the Splashing River.　He was very sad.
He was as sad as the wind that cried
round the wigwam in the cold winter.
He was as sad as the birds when they
could find nothing to eat in the snow.
He was still lost!

Then he saw something.
The root of a tree was sticking out
in the water, with a patch of green weed
floating beside it.

There in the weeds, against the tree root—
just within reach—
was a toy canoe!
It was a little one, made of birch bark.
It was his own—
Shining Moon's own little toy canoe!

"Oh!" cried Shining Moon in joy.
He bent down and took the canoe
out of the river.

He shook off the drops of water
and a piece of green weed.
He wiped the little boat dry.
His own little canoe!   He had found it!

Now he knew which way to go home,
for the little canoe
had stopped above the tree root.
So it must have sailed down the river
from that side.   So the wigwam must be
somewhere on that side, too.

Gladly Shining Moon
turned to the left
and ran along beside the Splashing River.
He ran and ran and ran, until at last
he came to the part that he knew.

"I'll soon be home now," he thought.
"It's quite a lucky day after all.
I've found my little canoe
and I've found my way home."

Darkness was creeping over the forest
now, but there, just ahead,
Shining Moon could see his wigwam.

Father was just home from hunting.
Mother was just saying,
"Have you seen Shining Moon?"
Baby sister was just tucked up
in bed for the night.

Out from the trees
beside the Splashing River
ran Shining Moon. His bow was slung
over his shoulder. His arrows
were tucked in his belt.
His little toy canoe of tree bark
was under his arm. He was happy again.

He was as happy as the squirrels
climbing in the trees.
He was as happy as the fish swimming
in the deep, grey water.
He was as happy as the birds flying
in the wide, blue sky.

Then, as Shining Moon
ran in through the wigwam door,
the shining moon,
after which he was named,
shone down over the forest,
to say goodnight to him.

The Lazy Donkey

There was once a donkey who was so lazy
that he didn't like having to do
any work at all. One day he had
to carry a load of salt for his master.
It wasn't very heavy,
but he went along very slowly.
As he didn't look where he was going,
he suddenly slipped
and fell into the river.

The salt was washed away
out of the bags, and when the donkey
climbed on to the road again,
he found his load had gone.
He was very pleased, and walked
on his way quite quickly, because he had
nothing to carry but the empty bags.

The next time his master put a load
of salt upon his back, the donkey thought,

"Ah! I'll go into the river again,
and get rid of the load."

He pretended to slip on the bank,
and he fell in the water.
Once more the salt was washed away,
and the donkey was left with nothing
to carry. He thought he was very clever.

"If I do this every day,"
he said to himself, "I'll never
have to carry anything at all."

But the load that his master gave him
the next day was not a load of salt.
It was a load of sponges.
Perhaps the master guessed that the
lazy donkey was playing tricks on him.

As soon as they reached the part
of the road that went beside the river,
the donkey slipped and fell in again.
He laughed to himself, thinking,

"Another load gone."

But when he tried to scramble up the bank
he found the load hadn't gone.
It was, in fact, much heavior
than it had been before.

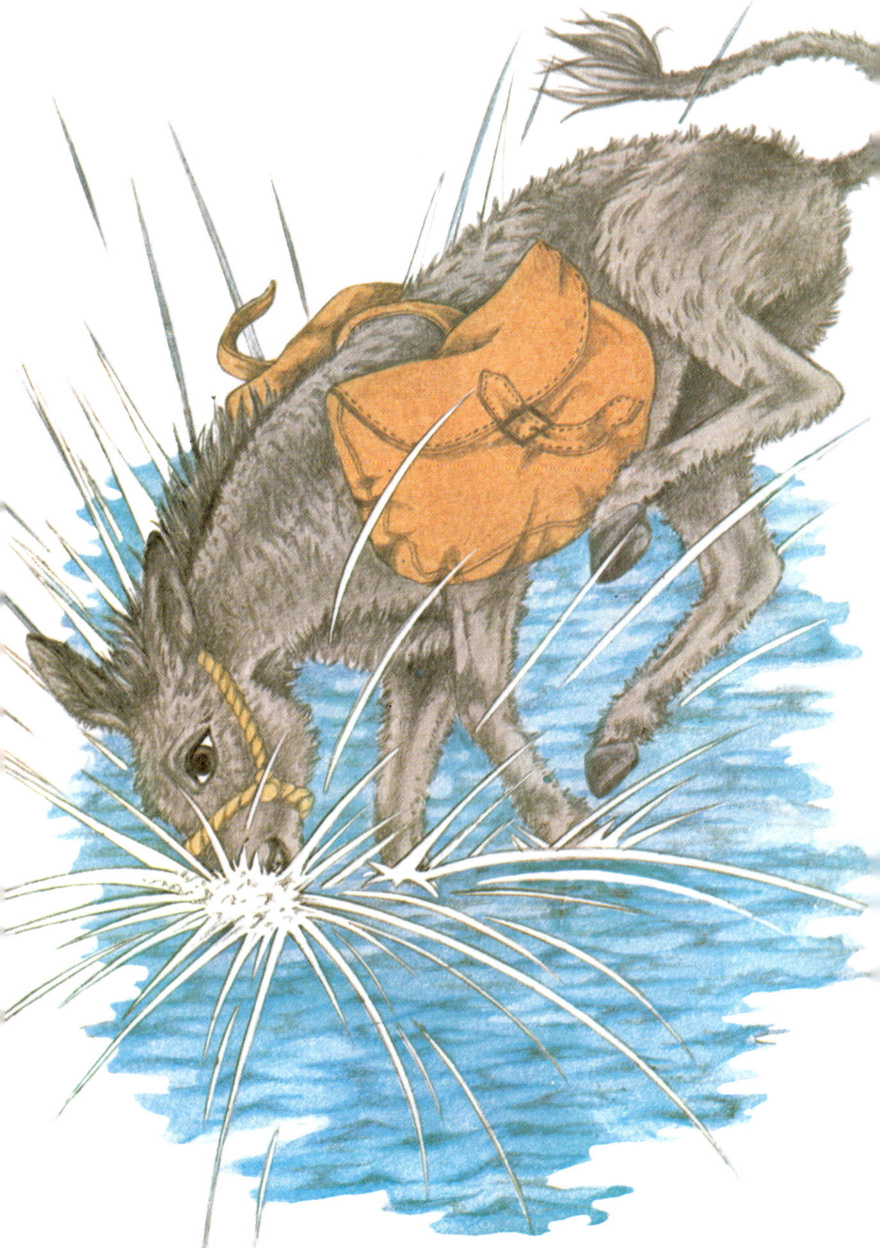

He went down into the water again,
but still he could feel the load.
In fact, it was so heavy that he couldn't
climb back on to the road again
until his master helped him.

   The donkey couldn't think
why the sponges hadn't melted away
as the salt had done.   He didn't know
that sponges soaked up water
and became heavier.
By the time he reached the end
of the journey, he was so tired
that he could scarcely move
under the weight.

   Never again did he try
falling into the river
when he was carrying a load.
In fact, after a while
he gave up being lazy,
and became a good, hard-working donkey.

Adapted

The Jigsaw Puzzle

Roger was waiting for a letter.
When Auntie Joan had come to town
in the winter, she had said,
 "How would you like to come
and stay on my farm, Roger?"
 "Oh, yes *please*. I'd love it,"
Roger had replied.
 "All right. I'll send you a letter,
telling you when to come.
The Easter holidays
will be the best time."
 Winter had passed now,
and the Easter holidays were
getting near. Roger was waiting
and looking every day for a letter.
It would be beautiful on
Auntie Joan's farm now. There would be
primroses in the wood. There would be
little lambs in the field, and
fluffy, yellow chicks in the farmyard.

And there *might* be a new little calf,
with wobbly legs and big brown eyes.
Oh, it would be fun!
If *only* the letter would come!

Every morning when the postman
knocked, Roger ran to the door.
Every afternoon when he came home
from school, he said to his mother,

"Is there a letter from Auntie Joan?"

And when Mother said no, he went
sadly to play with his baby brother,
or to do a jigsaw puzzle by himself.

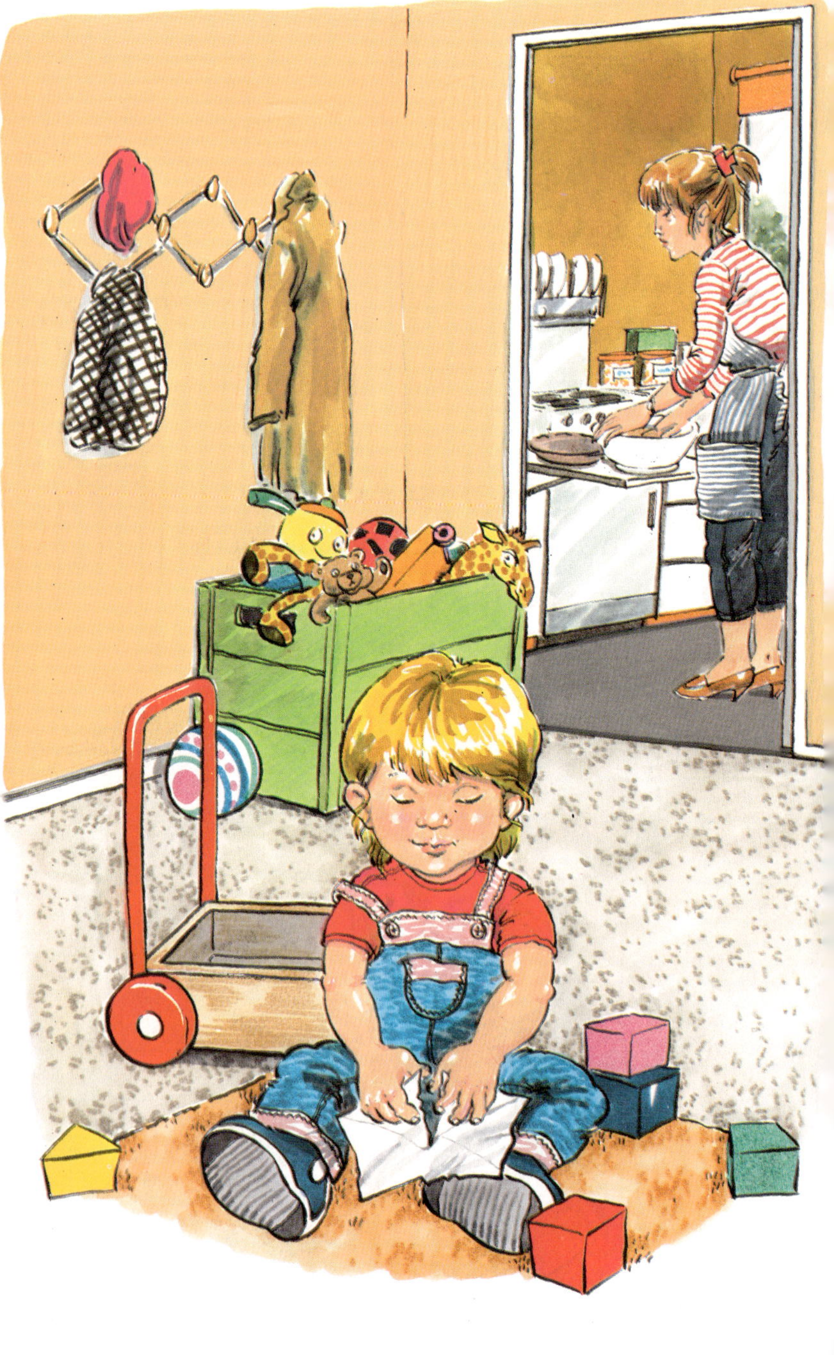

One day, Roger was at school.
Mother was making an apple pie
in the kitchen.
Baby was crawling up and down the hall.
Suddenly the postman came.
He slipped one thin letter
through the letter box, and went away.
The letter was for Roger, from Auntie Joan.

Baby crawled to the door mat,
and picked up the letter.
He sat down and looked at it.
He was at the age when he thought paper
was made for him to tear.
He liked tearing things.
First he pulled off one little corner.
Then he tore another little bit.
Mother was still in the kitchen,
making an apple pie.

"How quiet Baby is," she thought.
"I'd better go and see what he's doing.
I'll just finish the pie first,
and put it in the oven."

By the time the pie was finished,
Baby's work was finished too.
He had torn the letter
into little bits, and he had pushed
all the little bits behind a box in the hall.

When Roger came home from school
that day, he said,

"Mum, is there a letter
from Auntie Joan?"

"No," said Mother.
"Perhaps there will be one tomorrow."
But Auntie Joan's letter was lying
in little bits behind the box
in the hall.

"Oh, dear," said Roger,
as he sat on a chair
to do a jigsaw puzzle.

The next day when he came home
from school, he said,

"Mum, is there a letter
from Auntie Joan?"

"No," replied Mother.

"We break up this week," said Roger.

"Yes," said Mother. "I'm afraid she isn't going to ask you after all. She may be too busy."

"Oh, dear," sighed Roger. He felt very unhappy. It would be beautiful at Auntie Joan's farm now. There would be primroses in the wood. There would be little lambs in the field, and fluffy, yellow chicks in the farmyard. And there *might* be a new little calf, with wobbly legs and big, brown eyes. Oh, it would be fun!— But he wouldn't be able to see any of it. Auntie Joan wasn't going to write and ask him after all. (But Auntie Joan's letter was lying in little bits behind the box in the hall.)

Mother started getting tea ready at one end of the table. Roger started doing a jigsaw puzzle.

Just then Baby called from the hall.

"I think he's lost his ball,"
said Mother. "Go and find it for him,
will you?"

Roger got down from his chair,
and went into the hall. Baby sat by
the box, pointing to it.

"Has your ball rolled away?"
asked Roger. He knelt on the floor,
and peeped behind the box.
He put his hand behind
the box, and brought out the ball.

A small bit of torn paper
came out with it.

"I'll see what else is under there,"
said Roger.   Once more he put his fingers
behind the box.   This time he brought out
quite a lot of bits of paper.

"It looks like an old letter,"
he thought.
When he had brought out all
the bits of paper he could find,
there was quite a handful.

"Look, Mum," he cried,
running into the dining room.
"I found this behind the box in the hall."

"I expect Baby put it there,"
replied Mother. "He likes tearing up
paper, and hiding it in queer places.
Put it in the dustbin."

Then, just as Roger
was walking out with it, she said,

"Wait a minute. It looks
like Auntie Joan's writing.
Perhaps we'd better put it together,
and see what it is."

"Oh, Mum," said Roger.
"Do you think—? Do you think—?"

"It *might* be," replied Mother.
"You like doing jigsaw puzzles,
don't you? Well, this is a
real one for you to do."

Roger was excited as he sat
at the table. He and Mother
sorted out the pieces of paper.
Then they began to fit
the pieces of the letter together.

"Oh, it's coming right!" said Roger.

"It *is* from Auntie Joan, isn't it?
There's the name of her farm
at the top."

"Yes. It must have been under
the box for two or three days.
I expect Baby had a nice time
tearing it up, don't you?"

"It says, 'Dear Roger.'
Oh, please read it, Mum."

So Mother read,
"Dear Roger,

I hope you will spend
your Easter holiday with me.
I'll meet you if you can catch
the ten o'clock train on—"

"Oh, that bit is missing," said Roger.
"I *wonder* which day it says."

He ran into the hall again
to look for the missing piece.
He peeped behind the box.
He stretched his fingers under
as far as they would go.

But he couldn't find another bit.

"I'll move the box a little,"
said Mother.   It was a big box and she
pulled it with all her might.

"Oh, there it is!   There it is!"
cried Roger.   "It was stuck to one
of the feet.   Oh, look!
It says Friday, doesn't it?
That's the day after we break up."

So Roger finished the jigsaw puzzle
letter, and Mother read the rest
of it to him, right down
to the part that said,
"Love from Auntie Joan."

So Roger had his holiday after all.
There was so much to see at the farm.
There were primroses in the wood.
There were little lambs in the field,
and fluffy, yellow chicks in the farmyard.
There was even a new little calf,
with wobbly legs and big brown eyes!

The Rainbow Scarf

Granny Thompson always seemed
to be knitting. Every time Susie went to
see her she would be sitting
by the fire, her knitting needles going
clickety-click, clickety-clack. The knitting
gobbled up the wool and kept
growing and growing ever so quickly.

Sometimes Granny Thompson made things
for herself, but more often
she made things for other people.
She had made a new blue
cardigan for mother. She made several
new pairs of socks for father.
And she made a new white shawl
for Susie's baby brother, Simon,
and a lovely new red hat and
mittens to match for Susie.

After Christmas, when Susie went to
see her, Granny Thompson was sitting
by the fire as usual but she
wasn't knitting.
Susie missed the clickety-click,
clickety-clack of her needles.

"Oh dear," sighed Granny Thompson.
"I'm lost without any knitting to do.
I've finished all my Christmas presents.
And I've no more wool to
start something new until the shops
open again tomorrow."

"What about all the left-overs?"
asked Susie.   And she went to get
the bag where Granny Thompson kept the
little balls of wool that were
left over after she'd finished each garment.
Susie sometimes played with them and
made patterns on Granny Thompson's carpet.

"Oh, there isn't enough of
any one colour to make anything,"
said Granny sadly.

"You could make something in stripes," said Susie. "You could make a scarf—all different colours like a rainbow."

Granny Thompson laughed.

"Who would want a scarf like that?" she asked.

"I would," said Susie, "please."

"All right," said Granny Thompson. "That would be better than having no knitting at all. What colour shall we start with?"

"Red," said Susie, taking the ball of wool left over from her hat and mittens. "Red's my favourite colour."

So Granny Thompson cast on some stitches and soon the needles were going clickety-click, clickety-clack.

"Clickety-click, clickety-clack," said the needles greedily, and soon there was a blue stripe next to the red.

"Now yellow," said Susie.

Granny Thompson was cheerful again
now she had some knitting to do.
By tea-time the scarf had grown
quite long.   It was red and blue
and yellow and purple and orange.

"What a lot of colours," said Susie.

After tea Granny Thompson went on
knitting, clickety-click, clickety-clack.
Soon all the little left-over
balls of wool had been gobbled up
and the scarf was finished.

Susie said, "It's just like a rainbow, isn't it?"

And Granny agreed that it was.

Then Susie put the scarf round her neck.

"Ooh, it's lovely and warm," she said. "May I wear it to go home?"

And Granny said she could.

Susie was so happy she skipped all the way home singing clickety-click, clickety-clack, clickety-click, clickety-clack. Just like Granny Thompson's knitting needles.

Daphne Lister

Blackie

Mary and Tim stood on the hillside
where the rabbits lived.
There were deep holes
in the sandy banks, and stiff grass
in the rabbits' doorways,
but there was not a rabbit to be seen.
  Mary and Tim waited.
A bird sang a song,
and a little wind blew in the grass.
  "There's one!" said Tim,
and there it was, a small brown rabbit
with a bobbing, white tail.

It ran in and out among the grass.
Then it sat still for a moment,
and washed its face with its paws.

"There's another!" cried Mary.
"And another! Oh, look,
there are lots of them now!"

One after another, little brown rabbits
peeped out of their holes.
They ran in and out among the grass.

Mary and Tim could see
white tails bobbing everywhere.

"There's another one washing its face,"
said Tim.

"Those two look as if they are
talking to each other," said Mary.

On the road, not far away,
a motor car passed by
with a sudden noise. In a second,
all the brown rabbits had gone back
to their homes. Not one bobbing tail
was left on the hillside. There were
only the deep holes in the sandy banks,
and the stiff grass growing
in the rabbits' doorways.

"Oh!" said Mary. "They've all gone."

"We'd better go home too," said Tim.

Mary felt rather sad as she walked
home beside her brother.
She was thinking of Blackie.
Blackie was her own pet rabbit
and she was very fond of him.

He was soft and fluffy,
and as black as soot.   He lived in a box
with wire netting at the front.
It was rather a small box.
It was only big enough for him to take
three steps one way and three steps
back again.   There was no room for him
to run at all.   Mary thought how nice
it would be for Blackie to run about
on the hillside with the wild rabbits.
Perhaps that was what Blackie
wanted to do.   Perhaps he longed
and longed to be free.

   Soon the children reached home.

   "Don't forget to feed Blackie,"
said Tim.

   Mary took some cabbage leaves
and a fat carrot,
and went to Blackie's box.
He put his little nose
to the wire netting and wiggled it
up and down in the openings.

Mary opened the door and pushed
the food in quickly. Then she went away
to fill his drinking bowl with water.

When she came back, Blackie had eaten
the cabbage leaves and the carrot.
He was wiggling his nose
at the wire netting again.

"Would you like to come out
for a little while?" asked Mary.
Blackie wiggled his nose up and down
a bit faster.   Mary opened the door
and lifted him out.   Then she stood up
and held him in her arms.   He was
soft and fluffy, and as black as soot.

"Dear little Blackie," said Mary.

She held him tightly so that he couldn't
run away. But all the time
she was thinking how he would like
to run on the hillside
with the other rabbits.

"Mary!" came Tim's voice
from the path. "Mary! It's bedtime!"

"All right," called Mary. "I'm coming."
She put Blackie back in his box,
and closed the door.
She ran up to Tim,
and walked back to the house with him.

"We did see a lot of rabbits today,
didn't we?" said Tim.

"Yes," said Mary.

"Did you give Blackie fresh water?"

"Yes."

"I guess Blackie would like to run about
on the hillside with the other rabbits,
don't you?" said Tim.

"Yes," said Mary. "I expect he would,"
and she went to bed thinking about it.

She thought and thought.
She was very fond of Blackie,
but his box was small,
and he couldn't be really happy in it.
If she made him a bigger one,
it still couldn't be very big.
Perhaps Blackie longed and longed
to run about with other rabbits.
Perhaps he longed and longed to be free.

By the time Mary fell asleep,
she had made up her mind what to do.
Blackie should be happy.
She would set him free.

In the morning, Mary and Tim went
to the hillside once more.
Mary carried Blackie. He was soft
and fluffy, and as black as soot.
The children stood still for a while,
waiting to see if any rabbits would come
out of their holes, but none came.

Slowly, Mary put Blackie down
on the grass. He hopped about round
her feet for a few moments.

Then he hopped a little further away,
and came back again. Then he hopped
away a little further still,
and came back again. Then he sat down
and looked round with his bright
little eyes. Never had he seen
so much beautiful grass!
Never had he smelled such sweet,
fresh air. He gave a quick little hop
of joy, and then he darted
across the hillside. Mary and Tim
watched his white bobbing tail
going in and out among the grass.

"The rabbits may not like him, because
they're brown and he's black,"
said Mary, feeling afraid for Blackie.
She ran forward to try to catch him.
She wanted to take him home again,
where she knew he would be safe,
but Blackie ran up the hillside
and out of sight.

"Oh, dear," sighed Mary.

"I wonder if he'll be happy."

"I'm sure he will be," said Tim
as they walked home. "It's very kind
of you to set him free.
I know that if Blackie could speak,
he would say thank you."

★   ★   ★   ★   ★   ★

It was quite a long while before
the children went to the hillside again.
First they both caught colds and had
to stay indoors. Then it rained
for more than a week. But at last
came a beautiful fine day, when
the air was warm and the sky was blue.

"Let's go for a walk," said Mary.

"All right," said Tim.

They walked to the hillside.

"Perhaps we'll see some rabbits today,"
said Tim.

"Perhaps we shall," said Mary.

They stood on the hillside
where the rabbits lived.

There were deep holes in the sandy banks,
and stiff grass growing
in the rabbits' doorways.
But there wasn't a rabbit to be seen.

Mary and Tim waited. A bird sang a song
and a little wind blew in the grass.

"There's one!" said Mary.

"And another, and another!" cried Tim.

One after another, little brown rabbits
peeped out of their holes. They ran
in and out among the grass.
Mary and Tim could see
little white tails bobbing everywhere.

There were little brown rabbits playing
games together.   There were little brown
rabbits who looked as if
they were talking to each other.
There were little brown rabbits
sitting up and washing their faces.

   Suddenly a little black rabbit ran out
from a bush.   For a moment he played
a game with two or three brown rabbits.
Then he darted down the hill
to where the children were standing.

   "Oh, look!" said Tim softly.

   "It's Blackie," said Mary in a whisper.

The little black rabbit ran straight
up to the children, and stood
for one second at Mary's feet.
Then he darted up the hillside again,
and out of sight.

Mary couldn't say a word.
Her heart was too full of joy.

Now she knew that Blackie
was really happy. He had rabbit friends
to play with, and fresh green grass
to run upon. He was happy.
He was free.

"Good old Blackie," said Tim.
"He was trying to say thank you to you."

On the road not far away, a motor car
passed by with a sudden noise.
In a second, all the rabbits had gone
back to their homes.
Not one white, bobbing tail
was left on the hillside.
There were only the deep holes
in the sandy banks, and stiff grass
growing in the rabbits' doorways.

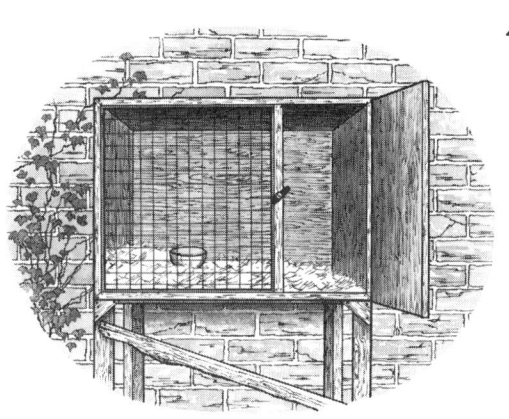

Adapted

Hot Supper

It was dinner time in the days long,
long ago, when people lived in caves
and killed wild animals for food.

Father had killed and brought home
a deer.   He and Mother
and the children sat round the fire,
holding great pieces of raw meat
in their hands (for no one yet had ever
thought of cooking anything).
They tore it with their strong teeth,
eating it quickly and hungrily.

"It's good," said Lok between bites.

"Good," said Baby, holding
a large bone in his fat little hands.
He was pulling the meat with his teeth,
just like a dog,
but Shan stared into the fire,
and ate nothing.

"Come, Shan," said Mother.   "Eat."

Slowly Shan picked up a lump of meat.

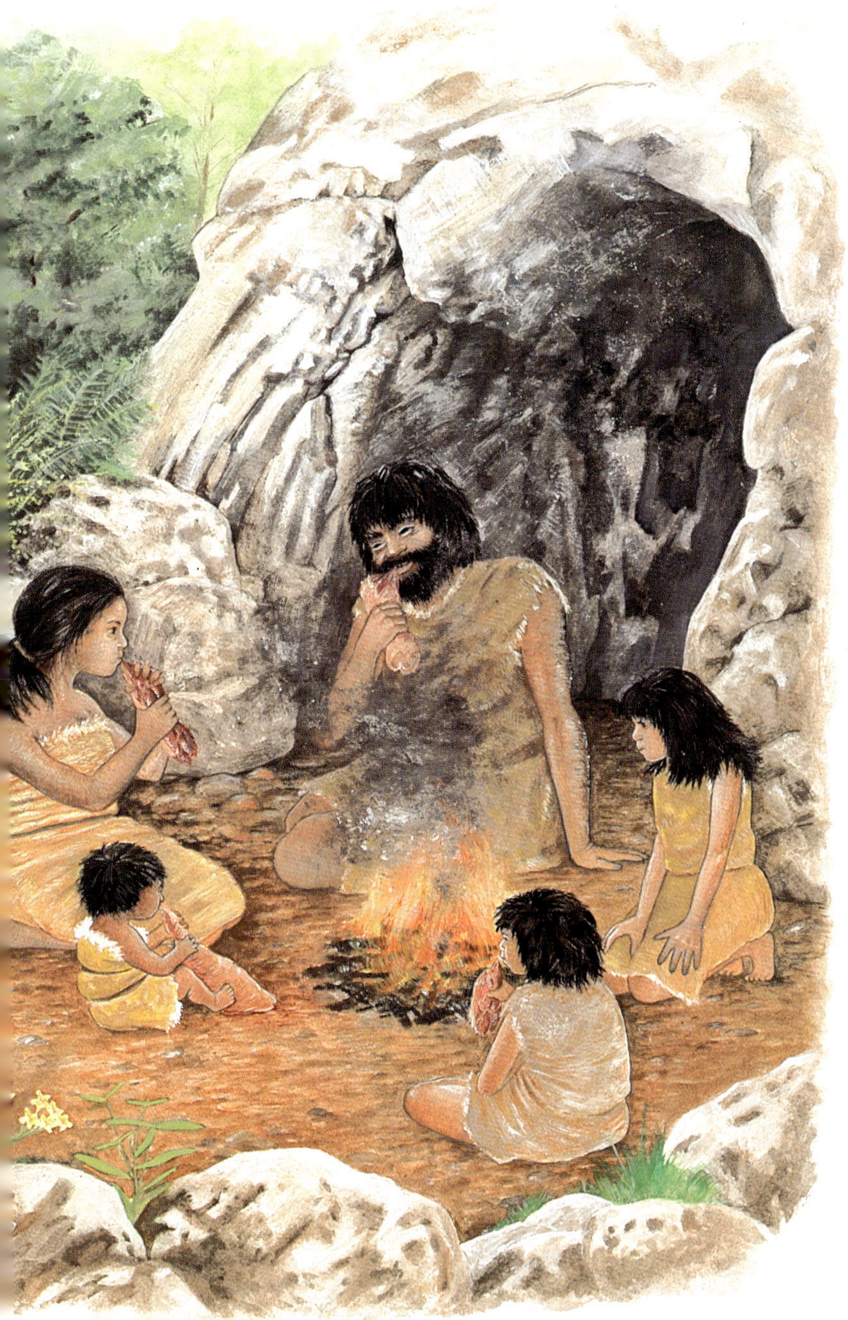

She nibbled a tiny bit from it,
and then put it down again.

"What's the matter, Shan?"
asked Mother after a while.
"Why don't you eat?"

"I'm not hungry," replied Shan.

"Not hungry!" cried Lok,
who always seemed to be hungry himself.

"You must eat your dinner," said Father.

"I don't like deer meat," said Shan.

"Don't like deer meat?" cried Lok,
who always seemed to like everything.

"I'm tired of it," said Shan.
"We had deer meat yesterday,
and deer meat a few days ago,
and deer meat a few days before that.
It always tastes the same—exactly
the same—and I'm tired of it."

The family stared at her in surprise.
Fancy anyone being tired of deer
—good, raw deer meat!

"Shan!" they all cried.

"Well," added Mother, "you must eat
something if you're coming out with us."
She tore Shan's meat in two,
and handed one piece back to her.
"There you are. Just eat that," she said,
but Shan only nibbled at it, and put it down.
She stared into the fire and ate nothing.

So when Father and Mother and Lok
and Baby went out that afternoon,
Shan was left behind. She watched them
swing through the trees,
jumping from one branch to another.
She watched Baby riding on Mother's back
and holding on to her long, tangled hair
with his small, fat fingers.
She heard the rustling of the leaves,
and Lok shouting goodbye as they went.
Then she was alone. She stared
at the fire again and said aloud,

"I'm tired of deer meat.
It always tastes the same,
and I hate it. I hate it."

She started to tidy up the grass,
throwing away the bones that the family
had left, and putting the pieces of meat
in a pile ready for supper.

At that moment a bird called so loudly
above her head that she dropped
the piece of meat she was holding.
It fell into the fire just near the edge.
Shan picked up a stick
to pull the meat out.

Then she laughed instead and said,
"The fire can eat that bit."
She was lonely without Lok and Baby.
She picked some berries from a bush
and put them in a row on a flat rock.
She played with them for a long while.
Then she saw that the fire
was getting low, so she gathered
some sticks to put on it.

As she threw them on, she saw that
the piece of deer meat was still
lying near the edge, among the glowing
ashes. It was black and burnt.
She gave it a poke,
and a tiny piece of it stuck
to the end of her stick.

Something smelled very nice.
She sat down on the grass,
with the stick in her hand.

She licked the end of it.
How nice it tasted.   It must be
the burnt deer meat that had stuck to it.
She felt suddenly hungry.   She pushed
the burnt deer meat out of the fire,
and let it cool a little on the grass.
Then she tore it to pieces with her hands
and tasted it.   How *nice* it tasted
—not a bit like deer meat.
She was really *very* hungry.

"Hot, burnt deer meat is nice,"
she thought.   "Much nicer than cold,
raw deer meat—and such a change."

No one had ever thought of *burning*
meat before, to make it taste better.
Shan ate the whole of the piece
that had been in the fire.
Then she let another piece
burn for a while, and ate that.

"Mother and Father and Lok and Baby
will be back soon," she thought.   "I'll
have a nice supper ready for them."

She chose some lumps of deer meat
from the pile. She pushed them into the
glowing ashes near the edge of the fire.
She left them to burn till
the sun began to sink in the sky.

Then she heard Lok's voice,

"Hello, Shan. Hello!" he shouted
through the trees.

Quickly Shan pulled the burnt meat
out of the fire with a stick,
and let it cool upon the grass.
Lok swung down from a branch,
and ran towards Shan.

Baby, who was half asleep, still rode
on Mother's back,
clinging to her long, tangled hair.

"I'm hungry," said Lok,
sitting by the fire.

"I've something good for you to eat,"
said Shan with a smile.
She handed him a piece
of hot, burnt deer meat.
He tore it with his teeth,
and began to eat it.

"This is nice," he said. "This *is* nice. What is it, Shan?"

"See if you can guess what it is," said Shan in delight. Then she gave pieces to Mother, Father and Baby. For a moment all was quiet while everyone tasted this meat. Then—

"It's good," said Father.

"It's the nicest meat I've ever tasted," said Mother.

"Good," said Baby, with his mouth full.

"What *is* it?" asked Lok.

"Don't you know?" said Shan. She was enjoying herself.

"No," replied Mother.

"It's the meat of some new animal that we have never tasted," said Father. "Have you been out hunting today, Shan?"

"Oh, tell us what it is," begged Lok. "It's *so* nice."

Then Shan told them.

She showed them how to put deer meat
at the edge of the fire
where the wood was red and glowing.
She told them how to let it burn—
not too little and not too much.

"Well!" they said.
"What a wonderful idea!"
Then they went on eating—
holding the burnt deer meat
in their hands, pulling it
with their strong teeth.

"It's good," said Father.
"It's good," said Mother.
"It's good," said Lok
and Shan and Baby.

And that was how
the cave people
came to have their
first cooked meal—
their first
hot supper.

Class 4's Summer Outing

Miss Mills clapped her hands for silence.
"Now listen to me, Class 4," she said.
"May Belle Watson, are you all right?"
"Yes Miss Mills," said May Belle Watson.
She sat on her own
half-way up the bus,
holding her picnic bag.
"Good," said Miss Mills. "Now! You all
know what I'm going to say
to you. This is our summer outing,
and I want every one of you
to behave well. Every single one of you."
"Yes, Miss Mills," said Class 4.
"And that means you too, Billy Jones,"
said Miss Mills. Class 4 giggled.
Miss Mills looked all round the bus,
and then looked at the list
in her hand.
"Billy Jones," she said. "I *have* ticked
him off. All the children are

here, driver. You counted them too."

"Twenty-two," said the driver. "All present and correct."

"Then where's Billy Jones?" asked Miss Mills sternly. There was a giggle from the girls at the back of the bus.

"Please Miss, he's under the seat," they shouted. May Belle Watson looked round in time to see Billy Jones crawl out from under a seat.

His tight red curly hair that his
mother had brushed flat that morning
was standing up all over like a
pot scrubber.   His jeans were scuffed and dirty.

"Billy Jones!" said Miss Mills.

"I dropped my mints," said Billy Jones.
"Would you like one, Miss?"
He held out some peppermints in a
very dirty hand.

"Er—no thank you, Billy,"
said Miss Mills, peering at them
through her glasses.   "Just sit down
please, and do try to behave."

"Yes Miss," said Billy Jones, smiling all over his freckled face.

The children cheered and waved as the black and orange bus moved slowly out of the school playground.

Some children in the other classes watched from the windows. Their summer outing would come later. The girls in the back seat of the bus waved.
Billy Jones flattened his nose against the window and made a cross-eyed face at the janitor as they pulled out.
Then they all settled down in their seats.

Class 4 was on the way for its
summer outing.

"Come and sit with me, Sharon,"
called Anne-Marie.

"No, she's with me," shouted Mandy.
"She's my best friend."

May Belle Watson sat on her own
and held on tightly to her bag.
She was new to the school.
She had only come two days before,
and nobody was her best friend.
Nobody was a friend at all.
She stared out of the window
as they drove through the small town.
It was much quieter and duller
than Birmingham.

"I don't like this place, Ma,"
May Belle had said the day after
they moved in. "It's boring!"

"Give it a chance, May Belle," said
her mother. "At least your Dad's
got a job here."

"But I left all my friends in
Birmingham," moaned May Belle.

"You'll make new ones," said her mother.
"And move over, you're sitting on
the cat there."

May Belle sat in front of the
television set with her legs crossed.
She hugged the cat in her lap.

"They're not a very friendly lot,"
she said. "Nobody wants to talk to you."

"Don't go saying things like that,
May Belle," said her mother, "until you know
for sure. You've only been at school
one day."

May Belle sat alone in the bus
and listened to the girls in the
back two seats. They were singing
pop songs now. She wanted to
join in. She knew all the words
of the song they were singing,
and could do it really well.
Dad said she looked just like
the girl on television.

May Belle sat back and
closed her eyes. Maybe she would be
a pop star one day. She sometimes
dreamed about what it would be like.

There was a loud squeaking sound
from behind her, then another and another.
May Belle opened her eyes and
looked round. Billy Jones was blowing up
a long yellow balloon and letting out

the air slowly. Miss Mills stood
up and looked round.

"What's that noise?" she asked, staring
round the bus. Billy Jones let the
balloon go and it flew
round the bus, turning and twisting,
bouncing off the lights and the
luggage rack. At last it flopped to the
ground in front of Miss Mills.

"Who does this belong to?" she asked,
picking it up. Nobody said a word.

"Billy Jones," she said. "Is it yours?"

"No, Miss Mills," said Billy Jones,
shaking his head. Miss Mills stared at him.

"I'm quite sure I saw you blowing it up,
Billy Jones," she said.

"Yes, Miss," said Billy Jones.

"Then it must be yours," said Miss Mills.

"No, Miss," said Billy Jones.
"It isn't mine. I found it under the seat."

Everyone on the bus
giggled. Miss Mills put the balloon

in her pocket and sat down firmly.
She was in a no-nonsense mood.
May Belle closed her eyes and
went on with her pop star dream.

A little later on there was a
shout from the back of the bus.

"Please Miss, Billy Jones says
he's lost his mouse!" The girls were
jumping on to their seats. Billy Jones
was crawling about on the floor again.

"Billy Jones, did you bring
a mouse?" asked Miss Mills, marching up to
the back of the bus. "Because if
you did we are all going right
back to the school. This very minute."

"Oh Miss!" shouted the rest of
Class 4. "That's not fair!"

"I mean it!" said Miss Mills,
and everyone knew that she meant it too.
Billy Jones stood up slowly and
looked at her. He said nothing.

Miss Mills made him turn out
his pockets. There was a very dirty
handkerchief. It looked as if he had
used it to clean his bike.
There was a piece of string,
a few football cards and a packet
of chewing gum.

"Now your anorak," said Miss Mills.
"And if I find there *is* a mouse,
back we all go."

Class 4 sat and waited with
fingers crossed while Billy turned out his
anorak pockets. One had a large
hole in it and the other was
full of old bus tickets and a
rolled up crisp bag.

"Did you have a mouse, or
were you just pretending?"
said Miss Mills.
She bent down to peer under
the seats. Billy Jones said nothing, but
he shook his head. Miss Mills
stood and stared at him very hard.
Nobody said a word for a long time.

"Very well," she said at last.
"But that's the end of your nonsense,
Billy Jones. One more bit of nonsense
and home we all go."

For the rest of the journey,

Class 4 behaved very well indeed.

At last the driver turned the corner into the road that led to the beach. Everyone crowded over to May Belle's side of the bus to look at the sea.

As Billy Jones and the others leaned across, May Belle looked up.

"Billy," she whispered. "I've got something of yours."

She opened her picnic bag just a little. But it was enough for Billy, Sharon and Mandy to see the little white mouse in the bottom. He was sitting there happily nibbling on a bit of sandwich.

"I'll give him back when we get off," whispered May Belle.

Billy Jones smiled all over his face. Sharon giggled and Mandy gave a little squeal of surprise.

"Shhhhhhhh!" said the others quickly.

"Hey!" said Sharon, as they were
climbing out of the bus,
"you're just great, May Belle!"

"Smashing," said Mandy.
"Come and have your picnic with us."

"If you've got anything left to eat!"
said Billy Jones, stuffing the mouse
back into his trouser pocket.
"Would you like a peppermint?"

"Yes, please," said May Belle Watson.
"Yes I would." She took a peppermint
from Billy Jones' very grubby hand.
Then she ran down to the sea,
laughing and joking with the others.

Moira Miller